Heaven is for Real,
and You're Going to Like It!

Heaven is for Real

for kids

_____

A Gift For

_____

From

Published in Nashville, Tennessee, by Tommy Nelson. Tommy Nelson is a registered trademark of Thomas Nelson, Inc.

Author is represented by the literary agency of Alive Communications, Inc., 7680 Goddard Street, Suite 200, Colorado Springs, CO 80920, www.alivecommunications.com

Cover and interior design by Koechel Peterson & Associates, Minneapolis, MN.

Tommy Nelson® titles may be purchased in bulk for educational, business, fund-raising, or sales promotional use. For information, please e-mail SpecialMarkets@ThomasNelson.com.

Scripture quotations are taken from the INTERNATIONAL CHILDREN'S BIBLE®. © 1986, 1988, 1999, 2005 by Thomas Nelson, Inc. All rights reserved.

Library of Congress Cataloging-in-Publication Data
Burpo, Todd.
 Heaven is for real for kids / as told by Colton Burpo to his parents Todd Burpo & Sonja Burpo ; illustrated by Wilson Ong.
     p. cm.
 Rev. ed. of: Heaven is for real / Todd Burpo with Lynn Vincent.
 ISBN 978-1-4003-1870-4 (hardcover : alk. paper)
1. Burpo, Colton, 1999- 2. Heaven--Christianity. 3. Near-death experiences--Religious aspects--Christianity. I. Burpo, Sonja.
II. Ong, Wilson. III. Burpo, Todd. Heaven is for real. IV. Title.
 BT846.3.B87 2011
 236'.24--dc23

                              2011025323

Printed in the USA

11 12 13 14 WOR 6 5 4 3 2 1

Mfr. Worzalla / Stevens Point, WI / October 2011 / PPO # 124345

Heaven is for Real
for kids

as told by
COLTON BURPO
to his parents,
Todd & Sonja Burpo

Illustrated by WILSON ONG

Tommy
NELSON®

A Division of Thomas Nelson Publishers

NASHVILLE   DALLAS   MEXICO CITY   RIO DE JANEIRO

Dear parents and grandparents,

When you look into the face of your little one, what is it you see looking back at you? For most the answer is simple— a miracle!

The love we give to and get back from a child is simply awesome. Nothing in our lives gives us the comfort and joy that a child can bring. But more than any other thing of value in our lives, the children God has given us need special care.

Children need someone to feed and watch over them, someone to pick them up when they fall, someone to run to when they are scared, someone to teach them about life as they grow up. Above all else, children need someone to teach them about Jesus and His importance for this life and the life to come.

If you have already read **Heaven is for Real**, then you know a little about our family and our son Colton's trip to heaven.

From the very beginning, Sonja and I were captivated by the simplicity and the power of the words that came directly from Colton about his experience. We both felt strongly that his innocent, childlike descriptions of God and of heaven needed to be shared with other children. Who better to connect with a child than another child?

Heaven is for Real for Kids is just that—a child's experience of his time in heaven, written in his voice, with his words— a book to be shared with other children.

But kids need more than just words; they need pictures too. The art was created under Colton's direction and drawn to reflect the experience he had during his amazing trip to heaven.

You may be surprised to find some details in this book that were not included in the "grown-up" book. Colton has actually shared so many memories that not all of them could be written in just one book.

We hope that you enjoy reading and sharing this children's edition of **Heaven is for Real** with your special little one. But beyond the simple enjoyment of the story, we pray that you'll join us in the certainty of knowing that, as Colton says, "Heaven is for real, and you're going to like it."

Not everyone gets to visit heaven and come back to earth, but Colton did! When Colton was almost four, he became very sick. His mom and dad took him to the hospital so he could get better, but while he was there an amazing thing happened. Colton closed his eyes, and when he opened them—

Jesus was with him!
Angels were there too, and then Jesus
had an angel carry him to heaven.
This is Colton's story.

Did you know that heaven is just
like the Bible tells us?
**It is wonderful,
and it is for real!**

"There are many rooms in my Father's house. I would not tell you this if it were not true. I am going there to prepare a place for you. After I go and prepare a place for you, I will come back. Then I will take you to be with me so that you may be where I am."

—John 14:2–3

Jesus is so happy when people get to heaven.
His smile is really bright, and His eyes sparkle.

When I looked at Jesus, I could tell how much He loved me.

Jesus really, really loves children!

While they watched, Jesus was changed. His face became bright like the sun. And his clothes became white as light.

—Matthew 17:2

Heaven is more amazing than you can imagine.

I could hear beautiful music and see lots of colors.
Big, bright rainbows are everywhere you look.
The streets are gold, the gates are made of pearl,
and shiny jewels are on the walls.

The foundation stones of the city walls had every kind of jewel in them.... The 12 gates were 12 pearls. Each gate was made from a single pearl. The street of the city was made of pure gold. The gold was clear as glass.

—Revelation 21:19, 21

Heaven is not scary—ever! There is no sun, but it never gets dark in heaven because the light of God is so bright. No one ever cries or is afraid in heaven. No one ever gets sad or mad.

Everyone is happy there!

The city does not need the sun or the moon to shine on it. The glory of God is its light, and the Lamb is the city's lamp. By its light the people of the world will walk. The kings of the earth will bring their glory into it.

—REVELATION 21:23–24

"Father, I want these people that you have given me to be with me in every place I am. I want them to see my glory. This is the glory you gave me because you loved me before the world was made."

—John 17:24

You get to meet a lot of people in heaven.

I saw Jesus' cousin John the Baptist, King David, Samson, Peter,
John, and Jesus' mom, Mary. I also got to talk to my great-grandpa
Pop. And my big sister was so excited to see me
that she wouldn't stop hugging me!

There are also lots of kids in heaven. Some are older, some younger, some taller, and some are shorter than I am. They get to play games and learn things from Jesus. Heaven is a really fun place.

You will never get bored in heaven!

> Jesus . . . said to them, "Let the little children come to me. Don't stop them. The kingdom of God belongs to people who are like these little children. I tell you the truth. You must accept the kingdom of God as a little child accepts things, or you will never enter it." Then Jesus took the children in his arms. He put his hands on them and blessed them.
>
> —MARK 10:14–16

Angels are everywhere! God's angels are mighty and amazing!
Michael and Gabriel are the biggest—they are as tall as giants.
Michael carries a sword that is about as big as my dad.

His sword is covered in flames and is really powerful.

The angels do lots of things in heaven. They help God and sing praises to Him.
They also deliver messages and protect people on earth. Angels are very busy!

"Be careful. Don't think these little children are worth nothing. I tell you that they have angels in heaven who are always with my Father in heaven."

—MATTHEW 18:10

Then wolves will live in peace with lambs. And leopards will lie down to rest with goats. Calves, lions and young bulls will eat together. And a little child will lead them.

—Isaiah 11:6

God, people, angels, and even animals are in heaven. All the same types of animals that are on earth are in heaven,

but in heaven they all get along.

You can play with any animal you like. I got to play with dogs, cats, elephants, and even kangaroos, but my favorite animals were the lions and Jesus' big white horse.

One of the most wonderful things about heaven is that no one ever gets sick or hurt there. No one ever has bumps or bruises or skinned knees. No one needs glasses or wheelchairs. In heaven, no one is old; everyone is young and healthy. And no one dies in heaven.

In heaven, you live forever with God!

I heard a loud voice from the throne. The voice said, "Now God's home is with men. He will live with them, and they will be his people. God himself will be with them and will be their God. He will wipe away every tear from their eyes. There will be no more death, sadness, crying, or pain. All the old ways are gone."

—Revelation 21:3–4

My favorite place in heaven is near God's throne. God the Father has a HUGE throne! Jesus sits on the right side of God. The Holy Spirit is also there. And there are angels and people worshipping God—I saw the angel Gabriel.

A little chair was brought in for me, and I sat by God the Holy Spirit. I was praying for my dad because I knew he was really worried about me.

God the Father and Jesus the Son will send the

Holy Spirit to help you when you pray.

They love you so much!

"I must not lose even one of those that God has given me, but I must raise them up on the last day. This is what the One who sent me wants me to do. Everyone who sees the Son and believes in him has eternal life."

—John 6:39–40

Jesus told me many things while I was in heaven. He told me to be nice to others and to talk to God in prayer. He talked to me about the markers on His hands and His feet from when He died on the cross. He did that so we could go see Him and His Dad in heaven.

The most important thing Jesus told me was how to get to heaven.

He said to believe in Him and follow Him. That makes God very happy.

Yes, I am sure that nothing can separate us from the love God has for us. Not death, not life, not angels, not ruling spirits, nothing now, nothing in the future, no powers, nothing above us, nothing below us, or anything else in the whole world will ever be able to separate us from the love of God that is in Christ Jesus our Lord.

—ROMANS 8:38–39

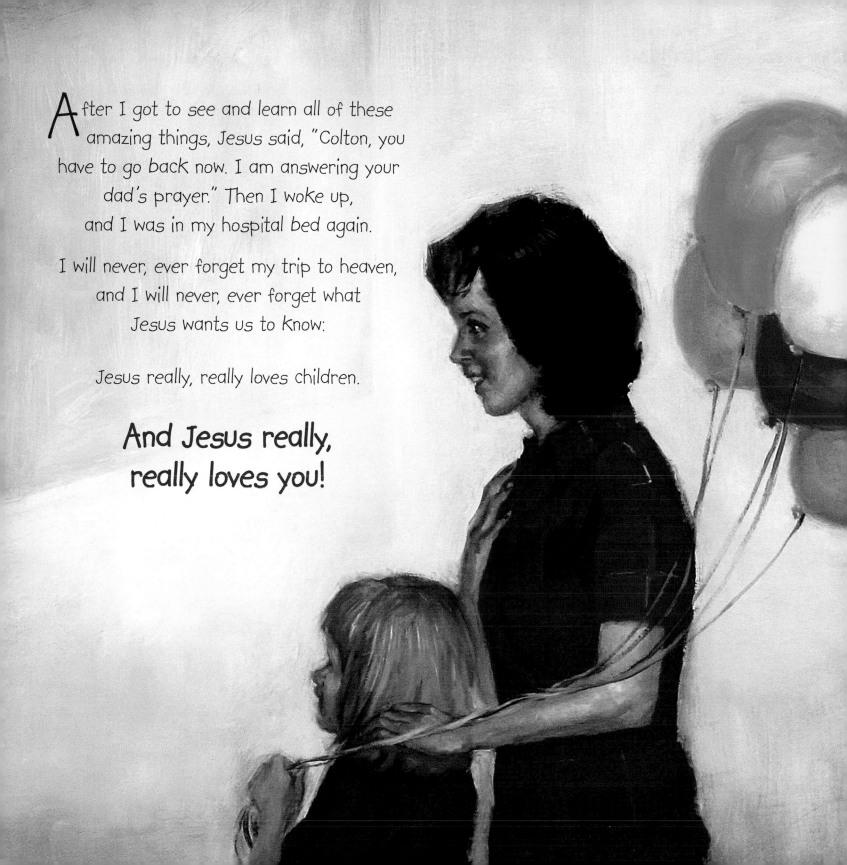

After I got to see and learn all of these amazing things, Jesus said, "Colton, you have to go back now. I am answering your dad's prayer." Then I woke up, and I was in my hospital bed again.

I will never, ever forget my trip to heaven, and I will never, ever forget what Jesus wants us to know:

Jesus really, really loves children.

And Jesus really, really loves you!

Heaven is for Real

1. ## What is Colton like today?
    As of fall 2011, Colton is twelve years old and still remembers most of his trip to heaven very clearly, but some details have faded. One day he hopes to become a musician. Colton enjoys listening to TobyMac and is gearing up for football, but he could do without the homework that comes with seventh grade.

2. ## Did Colton see more than what is written in this book?
    Yes. Not everything can fit into the pages of a book, but almost all of his favorite memories are included here or in the original book for grown-ups.

3. ## Have other people besides Colton seen heaven?
    Yes! God has allowed some people to see into heaven briefly. The Bible says Isaiah, Daniel, and the apostle John were all shown parts of heaven. The apostle Paul also talks about a man who visited the "third heaven," but he gives no name.

4. ## Can you get lost on the way to heaven?
    No. Jesus explained to His disciples that He would come back Himself to take His followers to His Dad's house. Jesus is preparing a place just for you, and He is going to make sure you get there, just like He did for Colton.

5. Is God on earth today, or is He just in heaven?

He is actually in both places. Before Jesus returned to heaven, He told His disciples He would send the Holy Spirit to help them. God is actually three Persons: God the Father, God the Son, and God the Holy Spirit, who is everywhere! Because of the Spirit, you never have to worry about being alone. Even though you can't see the Holy Spirit, He is always with you.

6. How will we know each other in heaven?

The Bible is unclear on this. But according to Colton's memories, both his sister and his great-grandfather Pop introduced themselves to him. Colton had never met either one, but they both obviously knew Colton. When Elijah and Moses visited Jesus on earth, they all recognized each other as well.

7. How do animals get to heaven?

Colton doesn't know. Although he saw the same types of animals he has seen on earth, he didn't learn anything about how they made the trip to heaven.

8. Do we really get wings in heaven?

As Colton says, "You get to choose if you want to walk or fly." Again, the Bible is silent on this issue. No verse says that our heavenly bodies will or will not have wings. Colton clearly remembers wings, and because he remembers so many other smaller details that align with Scripture, it would be very unusual for him to mistake something as obvious as wings on everyone's backs.

If you have more questions, visit us at www.hifrministries.org or www.heavenisforreal.net.

Dear God,

Heaven sounds so wonderful! I pray that You will be with me as I grow and learn more about You. Please forgive me when I mess up. Help me to be loving, kind, and forgiving. I want to follow Jesus in all things.

I love You, Lord!

In Jesus' name,
amen.

Colton's great-grandfather Pop in 1943 at age 29.

Colton in 2011 at age 12.

This image of Jesus was painted by eight-year-old prodigy Akiane. When Colton saw it, he declared, "That one's right."

Prince of Peace by Akiane, age eight.
www.artakiane.com